Wallasey Old Adverts

P. Davies

1935. Samuel Panter Brick were located at 228-232 Liscard Road. The shoe shop had already been in business for almost 100 years. Samuel had the honour of being the Town's Mayor in 1934.

1934. Pickfords Removals also opened another location at 31 Seaview Road.

1937. Edward's Fashion Wear

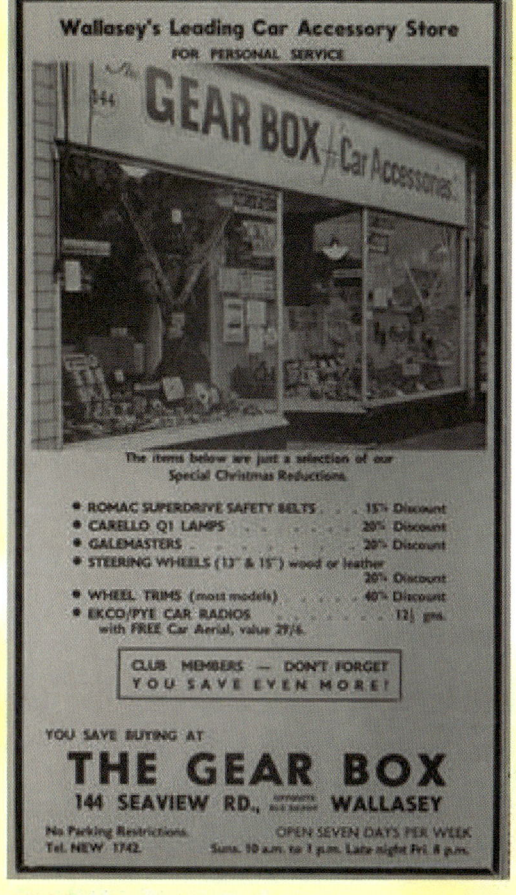

1967. The Gear Box

1953. S.S. Radio Services were established in 1936 and are still in business today in Mill Lane and are the oldest TV repair shop in Wallasey.

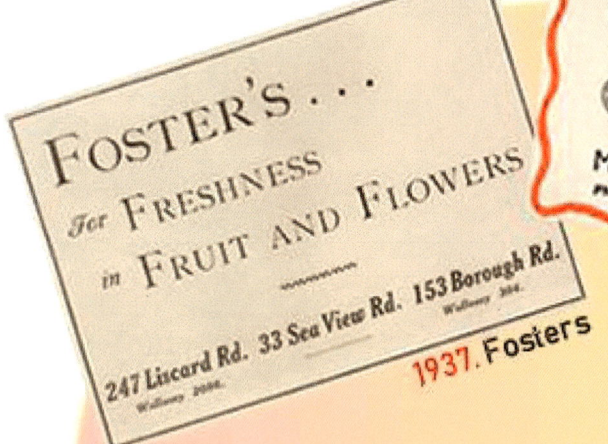

1937. Fosters

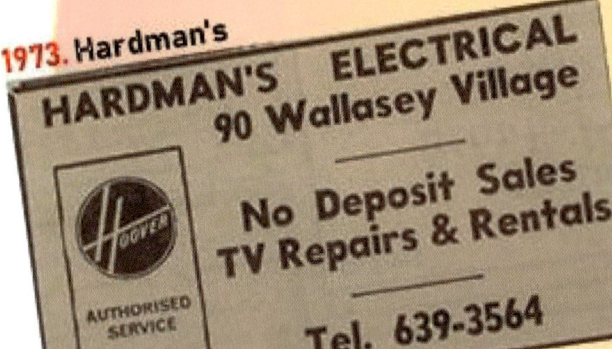

1973. Hardman's

1938. Situated at 34 Withens Lane was John **Bellis**, general contractor. The firm expanded and his two sons came into the business. They built a shop and house in 1894 with a yard attached. The house itself is red brick and still carries the letter "B" and the date built on the house plate.

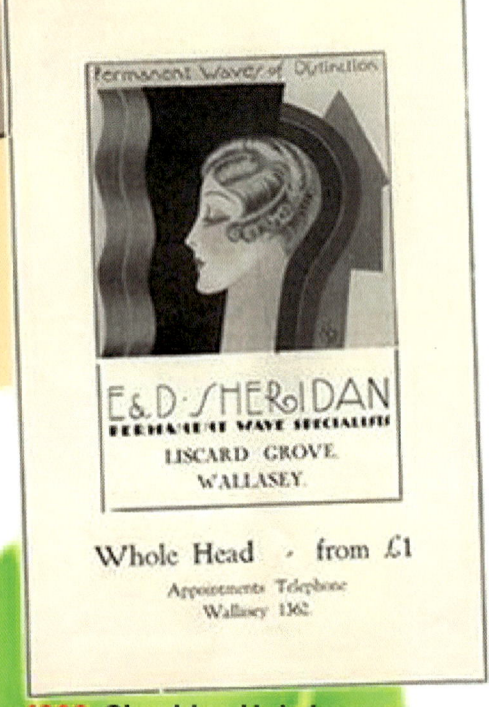

1930. Sheridan Hairdressers. The style of ladies hair fashion was defiend by Hollywoods iconic actreeses notably Bette Davies. Yours for only £3!

1925. The impressive building of Liverman's Furniture Store which once stood on the corner of Rowson Street and Victoria Road, New Brighton.

THE
GRAND HOTEL

MARINE PROMENADE
NEW BRIGHTON

BOLDLY situated on the sea-front and commanding magnificent views of the ever-changing panorama of river and sea . . . . an hotel of infinite charm, supreme comfort and personality.

DINE AND DANCE IN
The SPANISH RESTAURANT
DINNER DANCE NIGHTLY at 8 p.m.

Britain's Brightest Cocktail Bar

Open to Non-Diners

FULLY LICENSED.

For Reservations write or 'phone Wallasey 2243.

Appointed by the Automobile Association.

1953. The Marine Hotel, later renamed The Grand Hotel, opened on the Marine Promenade in 1845. In 1930 the hotel changed its name to the Grand Hotel. By the early 1990's the hotel was renamed as 'The Anchorage'. In 1996 the club closed following a fire and, after laying derelict for a number of years, was demolished.

**Windsors Garage
1935. and 1937.**

1966. Mobil Services

1960. Opened in 1953.

QUEENS PICTUREDROME,
POULTON ROAD, SEACOMBE.

General Manager - E. ANGERS.   Assistant Manager - F. THOMPSON.

Always a First-Class Selection of the

Latest and Most Up-to-date Pictures

Including Drama, Comedy, Instruction, Travel and Sport.

THREE HOURS' SHOW, Monday to Friday,
(7 O'CLOCK PROMPT).
SATURDAY CONTINUOUS PERFORMANCE, 6 to 10-30 p.m.

MATINEE, WEDNESDAY AT 3 O'CLOCK.

High-Class Musical Selections rendered each evening by
WALLASEY'S PREMIER STRING ORCHESTRA.

SEATS MAY BE BOOKED.   No Extra Charge.   Ring up 877 Liscard.

PRICES: 3D. 4D. 6D. 9D.

1914 advert. The Queen's Picture House in Poulton Road opened on 4th November 1911 and was Wallasey's first purpose built cinema.

The building was very attractive with a curved glass verandah and on the roof was an impressive looking dome.

The cinema served the local community until closing on 18th July 1959.

KENNY CAMPBELL, Ltd.
SPORTS OUTFITTERS.
CRICKET. GOLF. TENNIS.
Wonderful Selection of Bathing Costumes including Jantzen, Bukta, etc.
292 LISCARD ROAD,
LISCARD CORNER.
Phone Wallasey 252.

1938. Kenny Campbell (1892-1971) was a Scottish footballer, who played as a goalkeeper for both Liverpool and New Brighton as well as well playing for the Scotland International team.

AT YOUR SERVICE. CARDIGAN DAIRY.

1932. Standing on the corner of Mill Lane and Ashburton Road

CHESTERS Electrical Engineers
— only Address —
139 Victoria Road - New Brighton.
REGISTERED CONTRACTORS FOR
LIGHTING, HEATING and POWER.
Ring up WALLASEY EIGHT for your Electrical Requirements and Repairs.
Refrigerators, Cylinder Heaters and Cookers, etc.

1937. The electrical and music shop was situated at 139 Victoria Road. They sold a wide selection of gramophone records. They also once had a recording studio and Mr Chester even played the electric organ at various events.

1957. Milk Bar

MILK BAR
For a really good meal . . . . .
THE MILK BAR RESTAURANT
Catering for parties up to fifty   Special menu on application
LUNCHES   TEAS   SUPPERS   SNACKS
55 VICTORIA ROAD, NEW BRIGHTON
Tel - WALLASEY 1154

1960. R.D.C. Whitby

1972. Saunders Newsagents

1974. Cleary's Jewellers

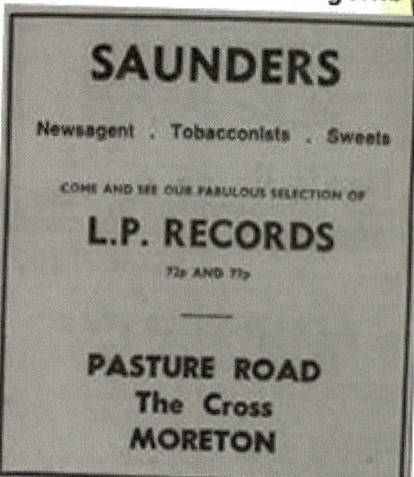

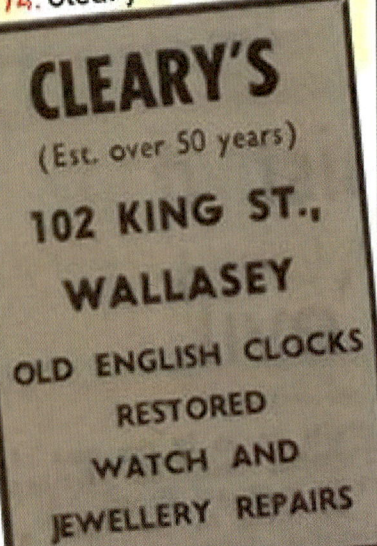

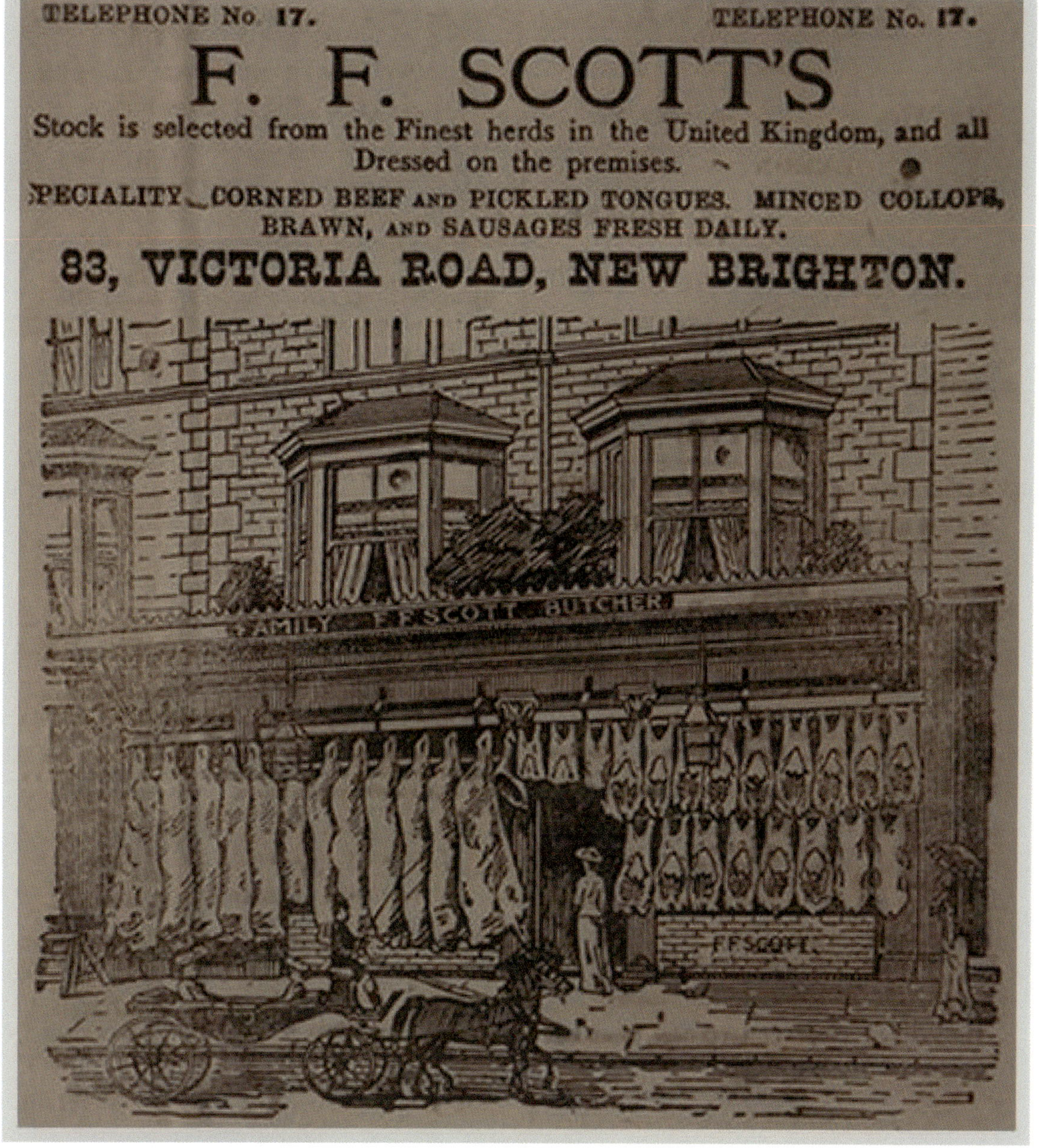
TELEPHONE No. 17.
TELEPHONE No. 17.
F. F. SCOTT'S
Stock is selected from the Finest herds in the United Kingdom, and all Dressed on the premises.
SPECIALITY.—CORNED BEEF AND PICKLED TONGUES. MINCED COLLOPS, BRAWN, AND SAUSAGES FRESH DAILY.
83, VICTORIA ROAD, NEW BRIGHTON.
FAMILY F F SCOTT BUTCHER
F F SCOTT

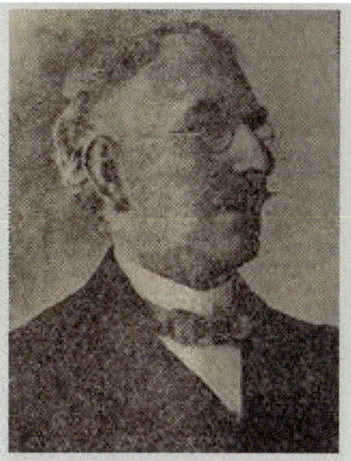

1909. Frank Fawcett Scott was born in Seacombe c1857 and opened his butchers at 38 Victoria Road (later renumbered as 83) in the late 1870s.

Frank served New Brighton on the Wallasey Urban Council and the Wallasey Borough Council. Frank also became Mayor of Wallasey between 1917-18.

STOREY & CO.
(J. G. STOREY)
BON MARCHE. NEW BRIGHTON.
TOYS :: FANCY GOODS : CHINA.

1946. Francis Storey was born in about 1845 in Ireland and opened his toy and fancy goods shop in New Brighton in the early 1870s. Later Francis would go on to represent the district in the Wallasey Urban Council, formed in 1894, which Francis was Chairman in 1903-1904, and on Wallasey Borough Council (founded in 1910). Between 1912-1913 Francis held the office of Mayor of Wallasey and in 1920 became the first Freeman of the Borough. Francis lived at 'Elmswood' in Atherton Street and even had a ferryboat named after him but sadly he passed away before the boat came into service. Meanwhile his second son John Gladstone Storey, born in New Brighton in 1882, would follow closely in his father's footsteps in the retailing business, as a fancy goods dealer in Victoria Road, and in politics as a local Liberal Councilor upon Wallasey Council. John, too, being elected Mayor of Wallasey for the year 1929-1930

1967

1926

1935. Byrom's had three cycle shops in Wallasey

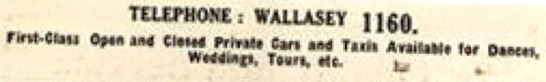

1934 Edward Harold Armstrong Taxi-cab proprietor

1953

1973

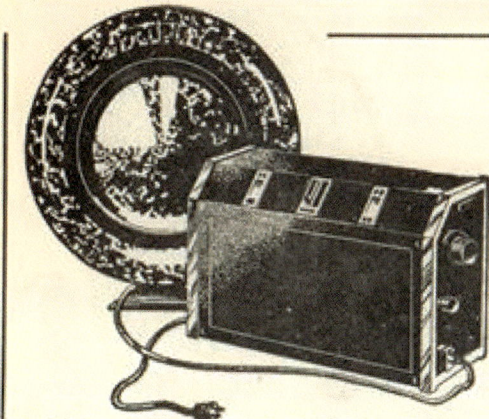

1931

1937

HOTEL VICTORIA

A.A.   NEW BRIGHTON.   R.A.C.

Premier Residential Hotel in the Wirral Peninsula. Delightfully situated. Hot and Cold Water in every room. Private Rooms for Weddings, Banquets, etc.

EXQUISITE LARGE BALLROOM AND SUITE AVAILABLE.

SPACIOUS CAR PARK.

For Terms apply to the Manager.

Bus S.   Telephone: Wallasey 2124 and 2125
Telegrams: "Comfort. Wallasey."

1935. The Victoria Hotel, later the Hotel Victoria, opened in 1837.

The Assembly Rooms were added in 1889.

In 1907 Dr. Hawley Harvey Crippen gave a medical lecture at the Assembly Rooms. Three years later he was the first criminal to be arrested at sea by the use of the Marconi Wireless. Dr. Crippen was hanged on 3rd November 1910 for the murder of his wife.

The hotel closed 1in 2004 and demolished in 2006. New flats occupy the site.

1933. Robert Yates Knagg had a number of jewellers in Wallasey: Rake Lane, Brighton Street and 256 Liscard Road. Robert would also serve as Mayor of Wallasey in 1949.

1903. Cycling would of flourished in the year of Warren's advert because in July 1903 saw the launch of the Tour De France bicycle race. Owning your own roadster became quite popular.

1935. John Kenna established the company in 1890. Today they are 4th Generation 'Kenna and Turner', Upper Rowson Street.

1930. The American Frank Winfield Woolworth first opened a store in the UK in Liverpool in 1909. There were almost 400 stores by the time of the opening of the Liscard branch. Another store would open later n Victoria Road.

With mounting competition from other high street stores and the increase in online shopping saw Woolworths close all its stores in January 2009.

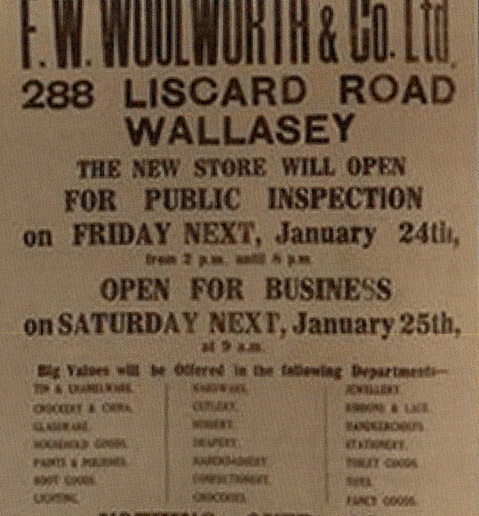

1956 advert below of The Nelson in Grove Road was originally a private house until Thomas Peers converted it to a pub. It was originally called Nelson Vault's after his wife's maiden name of Nelson. In 1935 the new one was built in stone, with Cotswold stone roofs and solid oak timbering and costing £25,000. The picture on the left is from the 1920s and shows the original pub.

"The Nelson"

GROVE ROAD   WALLASEY

A House of Distinction
Traditional Charm, Comfort, Hospitality
and
"The Trafalgar Room"

DAVENPORTS

extend congratulations to the
COUNTY BOROUGH OF WALLASEY
on celebrating the 50th Anniversary of the
granting of a Charter of Incorporation.

15 LISCARD VILLAGE ~ WAL. 280

EVERYTHING FOR THE DECORATOR.

PAINTS, VARNISH, STAINS, BRUSHES, BLOWLAMPS, DISTEMPER, GRAINERS, Etc.

THE NEW

Paint Rollers:— 'JUST ROLL IT ON'

SAVES TIME — PATIENCE — MONEY.

"CROWN" WALLPAPERS

THE VERY BEST THAT BRITISH CRAFTSMANSHIP CAN PRODUCE!!!

- **Modern Designs**
- **Exquisite Colours**
- **Plain & Patterned**

Visit our Showrooms for:—
BATHROOM and KITCHEN EQUIPMENT:
BATHS, TOILET SUITES, SINKS, ETC.
FIREPLACES, and COAL-SAVING ALL-NIGHT BURNER FIRES —— A SPECIALITY.

1953. Ellisons, Liscard Village

1948. Gandy Belt opened in Wheatland Lane in 1895 by Captain Maurice Gandy. He oringinally set up his business in Wapping, Liverpool some sixteen years earlier but decided to move the factory to Seacombe.

He began his earlier life as a seafarer but after being shipwrecked he decided to retire and became a ship-owner and cloth manufacturer in 1865.

However, not happy with the venture, Captain Gandy longed to start something new. His Gandy Belts works had branches all over the world.

There was an unfortunate serious fire at the works on 18th February, 1927. The fire caused £250,000 in damages.

The picture below shows inside the Gandy Belt factory in 1907.

1937 Advert. At the junction of Rake Lane and Magazine Lane was once a drapers shop owned by Benjamin Stroude who was also a member of the Wallasey Council.

The building was built in 1891 and still takes the name of Stroude's Corner today.

1908 advert. The New Brighton Hotel was originally a small private house and was later coverted to a pub. The hotel would go through many name changes, including Neptune Hotel, Lacey's and Pegg Gadfly's

1972 advert. The Tavern was originally St. James School which opened in 1847. The school catered for the children of New Brighton. In 1960 the school was converted into a nightclub called The Tavern. By 2015, owing to complaints from local residents 'The Tav' closed in 2015.

1915 advert. The Pilot Boat House was built originally in 1747 as a cottage. There was once a boat house attached to the pub where the river pilots kept their boats.

See the wonderful Displays of
PIANOS · TELEVISION · RADIO & HOME ELECTRICALS
at **STROTHERS**

★ Television ★

You'll always find a full range of models by leading makers at Strothers. More and more "People with Vision" are taking advantage of Strothers "All in" terms whereby, for a low deposit, and weekly payments from as little as 16/11d., you can have the Television set of your choice on terms that include the **AERIAL** and **TWO YEARS' COMPLETE MAINTENANCE**, including replacement of tubes, valves and all components.
IMMEDIATE INSTALLATION.

Come and see the fine new T.V. sets at our popular Television demonstrations in the Television Lounge.

★ Pianos ★

No Deposit FROM **10/-** WEEKLY

A good piano is a lasting source of pleasure and gives added distinction to your home. Come and inspect the wide range of beautiful models, from the popular "Minipiano" to superb Baby Grands, on display in our new store.

All Strothers' pianos are guaranteed for ten years, and you can purchase, without deposit, on terms from as little as 10/- weekly.

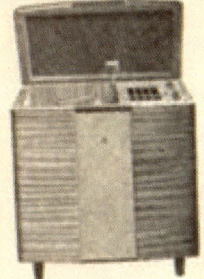

£5 DEPOSIT

★ Radiograms ★

A wide selection of the latest 3-speed console and table models playing both L.P. and standard recordings. Wonderful tone, fidelity and range. All available on Strothers "All-in" weekly terms which include two years' complete maintenance of all valves and components. Come and see and hear them.

WASHING MACHINES : REFRIGERATORS : VACUUM CLEANERS
RADIATORS : ELECTRIC FIRES : CONVECTOR HEATERS
FOOD MIXERS : STEAM or DRY IRONS : ELECTRIC BLANKETS
— AND ALL HOME ELECTRICAL AIDS

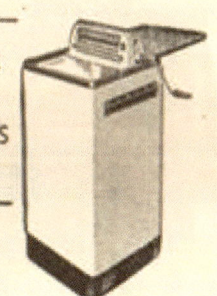

STROTHERS
CORONATION BUILDINGS, WALLASEY RD.
WALLASEY

Tel. Wall. 2296   And at Heswall and West Kirby.

1954 Advert. Robert Alfred Strothers, 8 Seaview Road

Chelsea Reach

Merseyside's most exciting DISCO PUB

open every night till 12 midnight

FREE ADMISSION MONDAY (including Supper), TUESDAY, WEDNESDAY, THURSDAY.

ONLY 35p FRIDAY & SATURDAY.
SUNDAY 20p, including FREE supper
Every Night FREE before 8.30 p.m.

Dancing EVERY night to Merseyside's top team of D.J.s BEAT THE BUDGET!

Despite the Budget increases our prices have NOT been raised!!!

Party Suites available for all functions.

TOWER PROM, NEW BRIGHTON. 051-639 1000
(wcf)

1976 advert. Chelsea, Tower Promenade.

ALBION HOTEL

A First-class Residential Hotel
(Fully Licensed).

PLEASANTLY SITUATED A FEW MINUTES' WALK FROM THE SHORE, GOLF LINKS, THEATRES AND STATION
(with connection to all Main Lines).

Hot and Cold Water in each Bedroom - Central Heating

MONTPELLIER CRESCENT,
NEW BRIGHTON.

For Tariff apply to the Manager.

Bus 5.   Telephone: Wallasey 1832

1948 advert. The Albion Hotel was built by one of the Earls of Derby in about 1835. Over the years the building was altered. New wings and bedrooms were added and the garden was reduced.

The pub closed in 2000 and the building was converted to flats.

Liscard Road Town Centre Trade Directory of 1967

259-261 The Tower Hotel
277-278 Cordon Bleu Freezer Food Centre
279-281 Lotus Footwear
283 Currys Electrics
285 Hiltons Footwear
287 Rediffusion TV Rentals
289 John Menzies Stationers, Books & Toys
291-295 Littlewoods
297 Haberdash
299 Sayers
301-305 Marks & Spencer
307 Trueform Footwear
309 Burton Tailors
311-313 Julian Swift Furnisher & Carpets

1972

236 Midland Bank
238-242 Stars Ladieswear
244 D.E.R Footwear
246 J. Toner Footwear
248 Woodhouse Furnisher & Carpets
250-252 John Blundell Ltd House Furnishers
254-258 Liscard Pantry Café
260-272 Birkenhead & District Co-Op
274 Timpsons Footwear
276 Thomas Cook Travel Agent
278-280 Boots Chemist
282 Johnsons Dry Cleaners
284 Coombes Boot Repairers
286-288 Woolworths
290 Maypole Dairy Butter Makers

1934.

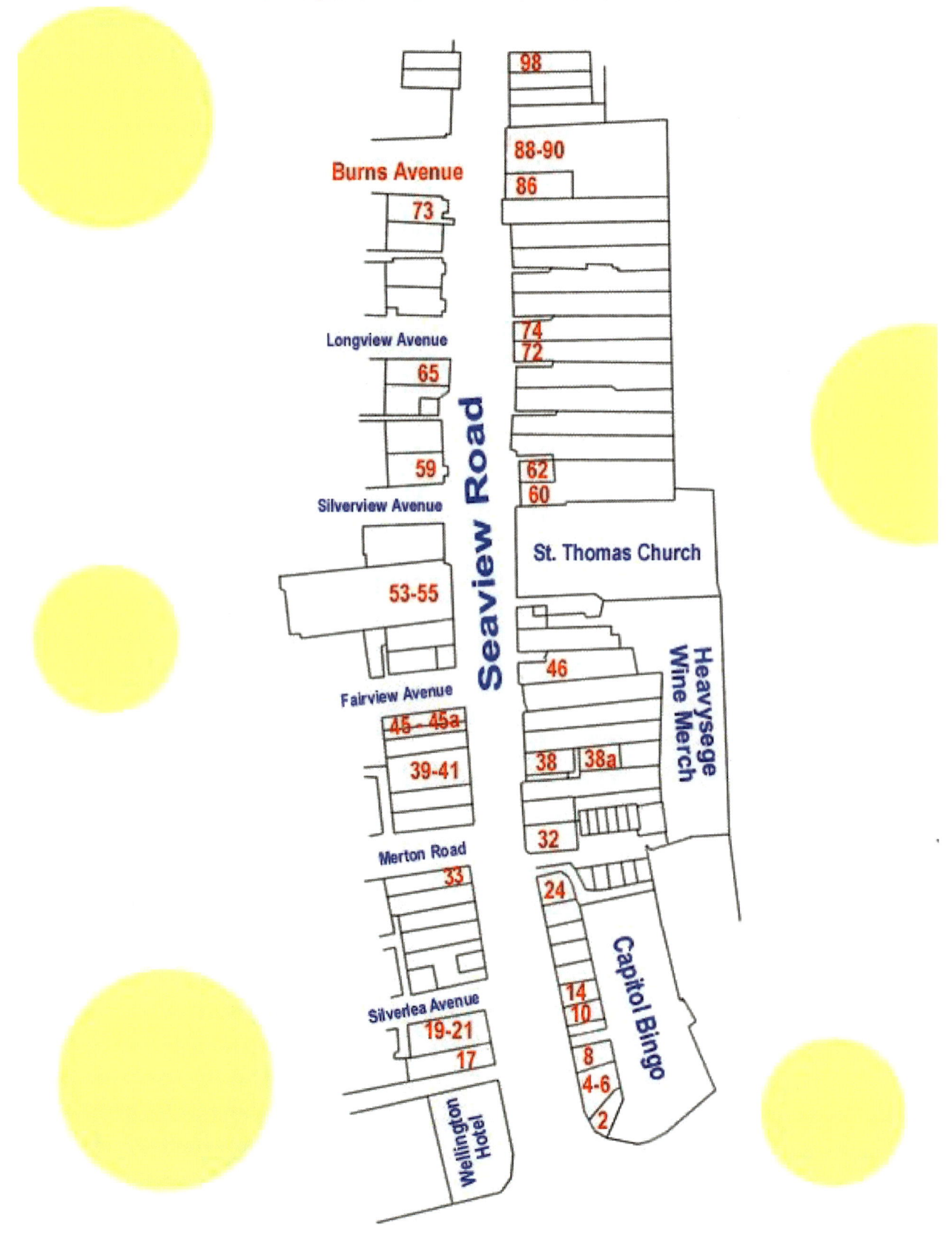

Seaview Road Trade Directory, 1967

2 Lavells Confectioners
4-6 James Horn Ltd Outfitters
8 North Western Gas Board

Capitol Buildings:
10 Archibald Lane Estate Agents
10 State Assurance Co. Ltd
10 National Savings Committee
10 Scottish Legal Life Assurance Society

12 Heavysege Ltd. Wine Merchants
14 B.J. Stroude & Co Drapers
16 Robert Knagg & Son Fancy Goods Dealers
18 Rediffusion
20 Joan Hallwood Milliner
22 The Coffee Roast Restaurant
24 Greenline Fruit & Veg
32 Paige Ladies Wear
34 Crown Wallpaper & Paint
36 Wearry Footwear
38 Laurie Fancy Goods
38a Benson Carpets
40 Eric K. Laurie Ltd Jewellers
42 P. Toner Toys & Cycles
44 Ryder House Knit/Wool & Knit Wear
46 L. Cowan Menswear
50a Barbara's Ladies Hairdresser
50 Heaveysege Ltd Wine & Spirit Merchants
60 Fells's Furniture
62 L.R Jervis Ltd Electrical Contractors
64 James Lear Ltd Outfitters
66 E.L. Barry Dentist
68 Junior Age Children's Wear
70 Rayner & Keeler Opticians
72 Clements Ladies Hosiery
74 Wallasey News Office
76 M. Pemberton Butchers
78 Koffee & Cards
80 Washgay Laundry
82 Spooners Fried Fish Dealer
84 Mrs. Lillian Farrer Furrier
86 Mrs. Blanche Ellison Florist
88-90 Woods Motor Showrooms
92 John Ryan Vaughan Newsagent
94 Cecil Triplett Fishmonger
96 W & D Harper Bakers
98 Vogue Ladieswear

17 Huddersfield Building Society
19-21 Lloyds Building Society
23a Wilson & Sons Estate Agents
23b Mr. M.J. Moss Drapers
25 Liverpool Investment Building Society
27 W. Brereton Butchers
29 Reval Ltd. Ladies Wear
31 Pickfords Travel Agency
33 F. Foster Fruit & Veg
35 Wrights Ladies Wear
37 Richard Quilliam Butchers & Provisions
39-41 Liscard Trustee Bank
43 F. Manning Health Food
45 G. Coleman Tailors
45a M.J. Moss Childswear
47 Finlasons Opticians
49-51 Rene's Café
53-55 Lennon's Supermarket
57 Cohen's Furniture
59 A.Antoni Fried Fish Dealer
61 British Furnishing Company
63 Cain Bros. Ltd Coal Merchants
65 C. Steele Vets
67 Cokers Nurseries Flowers and Seeds
69 Pringles Knit & W-ool
71 Mason Howley Ladies Hairdressers
73 Ellsons Tea Blenders
79a Murray Gould Tailor
79b C.M Twidale Sporting Goods

1972 advert

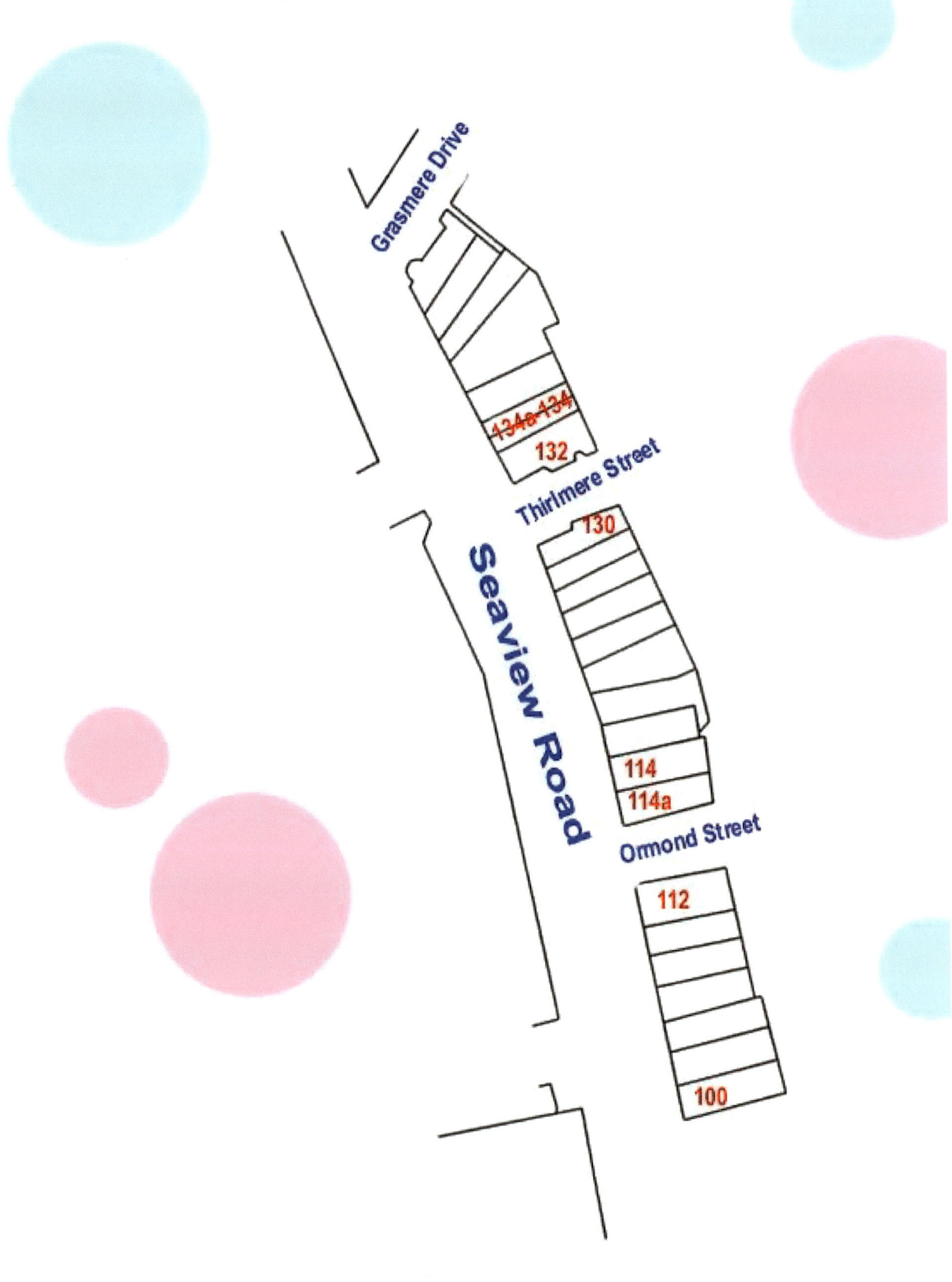

Seaview Road Trade Directory, 1967

100 Edna Rands Ladies Hairdressers
102 Central Dyers & Cleaners
104 Gayline Ladieswear
106 Vacant
108 L&Y Kirby Ladies Hairdressers
110 W.J Bampton Fireplaces
112 Harvey's Fruit & Veg & Florist
114a Millman & Partners Estate Agents
114 D.G. Igoe & Co Electrical Engineers
116 Stanley Johnson Plumber
118 Fancy Goods Ltd
120 Antoni's Ladies Hairdressers
122 Walter & Read Newsagents
124 Harold J. Twinn Stamp Dealer
126 S. Demetlieu Fried Fish Dealer
128 Mackies Off Licence
132 Seyferth & Sons Hardware Dealers
134a J.C. Eames Second Hand Goods
134b Wallasey Radio Tv Repairers
136 Christian Science Reading Room
138 A. Norman Milly & Line
140 Albert Bosely Tobacconist
142 Scotty's Lampshade Dealers
144 Gear Box Car Accessories

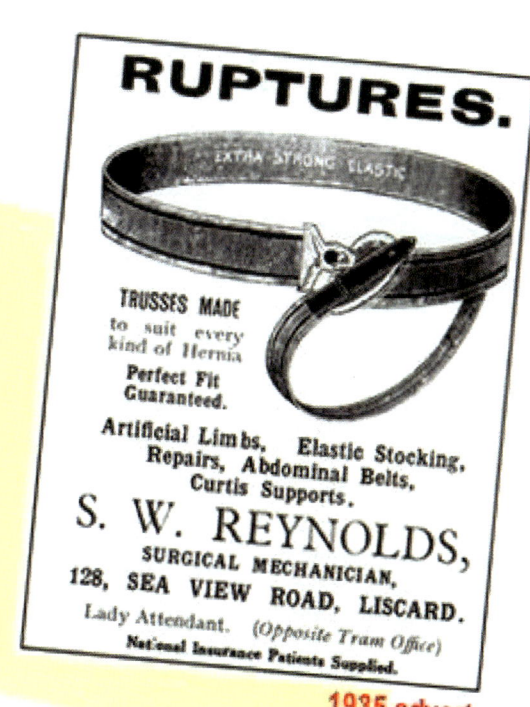

1935 advert

1929 advert.

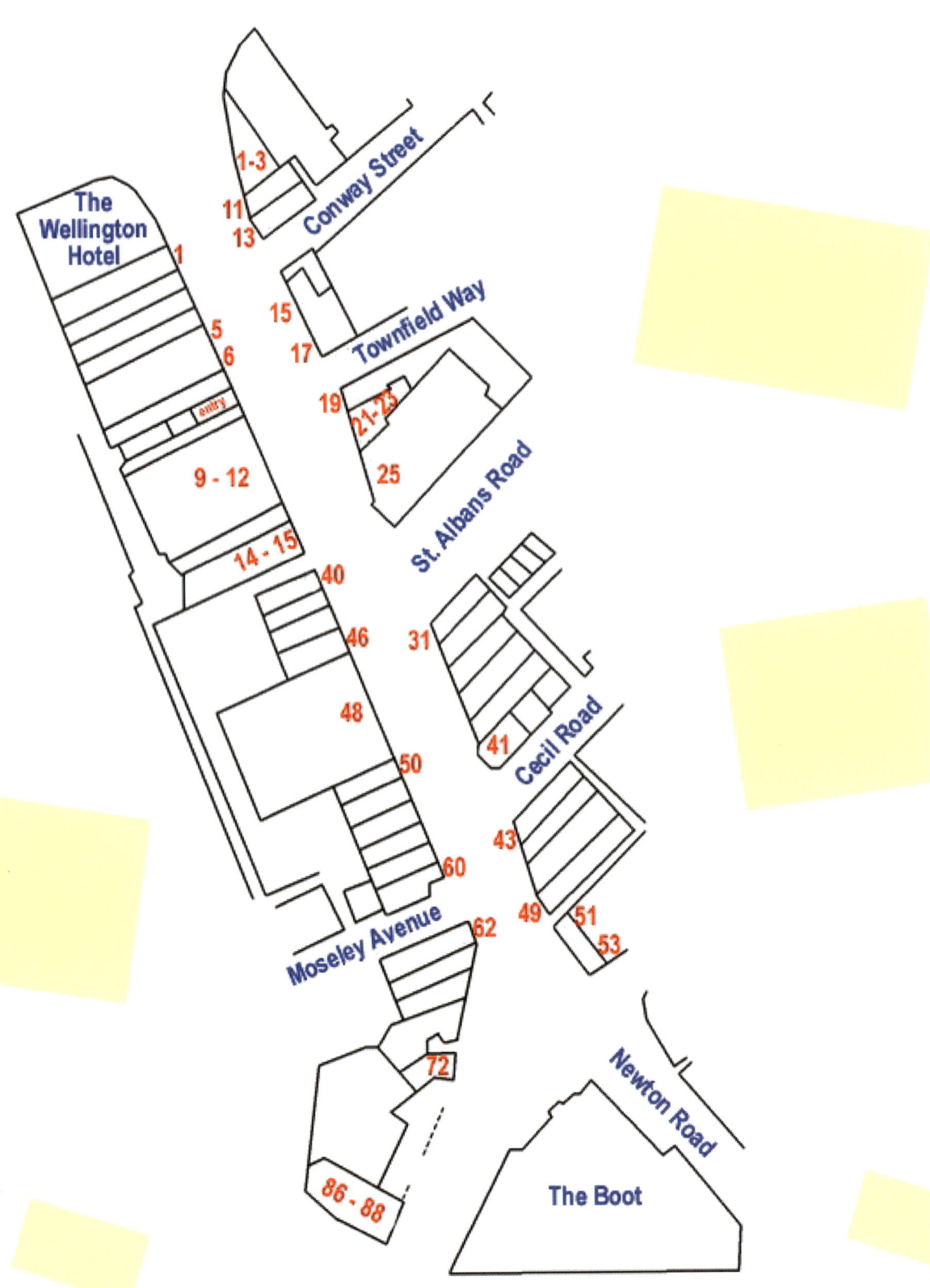

Wallasey Road Trade Directory, 1967

Wellington Hotel

Coronation Building:
1 New Dynasty Restaurant
2 Bookland Books & Stationary
3 Fludes Carpets
4 McLachlans Tobacco & Confectionary
5-6 Birkenhead District Co-Op Grocer
7 H.T Spence
National Assistance Board
H.M Inspector of Taxes
8 Famous Army Stores
9-12 Strothers Electrics
13 Cousins Restaurant
14-15 J. McKenzie Radio, TV & Electrics

40 Reece's Baker
42 Granada TV Rentals
44 Kyle Wallpaper & Paint
46 Marilyn Ladies Fashion
48 Safeway Grocer Supermarket
50 Spencer Dry Cleaners
52 Wrights Ladies Fashions
54-56 Clarendon Furnishers & Carpets
58 Radio Rentals
60 Vacant
62 Black Menwears
64 Bellis Tobacconists/Confectioners/Toys
66 Hardings Furnishing Removers
68 Charlton Butchers & Provisions
72 Boughey Estate Agents
Pinnington Bros Garage & Services
86-88 Strothers Office TV Supplies

1-9 J.Swift Home Furnishers
11 Minn & Co. Paint Manufacturers
13 Bellwood Jewellers
Merseyside & North Wales Electricity Board
19 Pritchard & Son Ltd Removals
21-23 Vacant
25 Vacant (formerly Castle Hotel)
31-33 Westminster Bank Ltd
35 Pritchard Offices
37 P. Bailey Tobacconists
39 W.H. Trace & Son Ltd Electrical Contr.
41 National Coal Board
43 Royal London Mutual Insurance Society
45 R. Eskay Glass & Chinaware
47 Truplett Butchers
49 Lin Hong Restaurant
51-53 Bell Joynson Solicitors
Boot Inn

1968

Shops In Wallasey Road, 1967

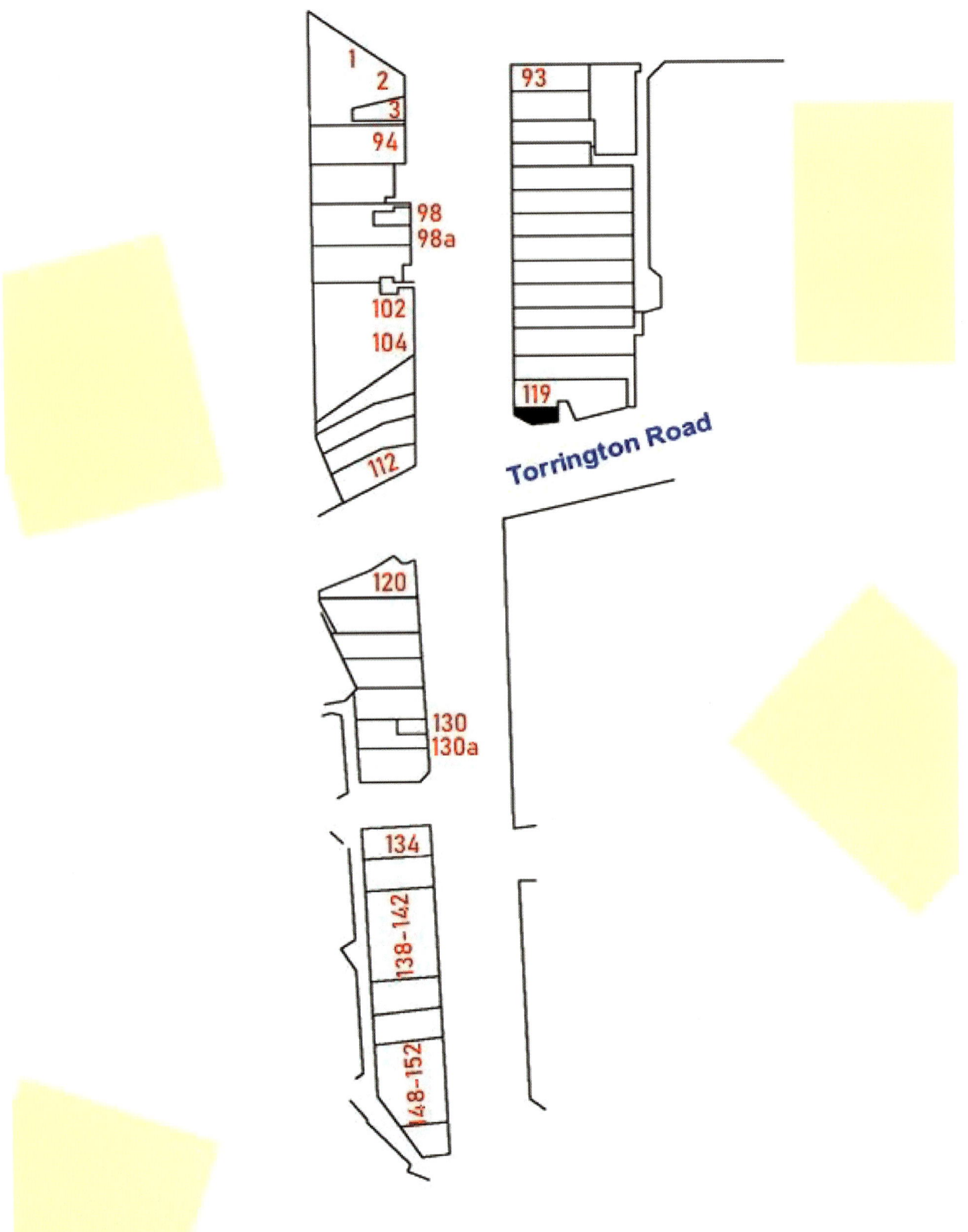

Wallasey Road Trade Directory, 1967

94 Motherland Prams & Toys
96 C.M Briggs Opticians
98 Betty's Ladies Hairdressers
98a E.G. Raddish Estate Agents
100 J. McCulloch Sports Equipment & Fishing Tackle
102-104 Leicester's Print, Stationary & Art Materials
106 Hardy's Menswear
108 V. Warburton Ladies Outfitters
110 Greenline Fruit & Veg
112 Harold Taylors Bakers
120 N. Burrows Fried Fish Dealer
122 William Brown Hardware Dealer
124 Vacant
126 F.D. & M.M England Drapers
128 Vaughan Newsagents
130 Hawkers & Hunters Electrical Contractors
130a Mary B. Keen Florist
132 Charles Plant Grocers
134 Oxfam
136 Vacant
138-142 Birkenhead & District Co-Op Society
144 Cheetham Ladies Hairdressers
148-152 Wilkinson Wallpaper
154 Johnsons Dry Cleaners

1973

93 Compton & Sons Estate Agents
95 Central Laundry Dry Cleaners
97 C.B. Collinson Estate Agents
99 Tudor Gift Shop
101 Wilbraham Turf Commission Agents
103 Barber & Co. Wine Store
105 W.E. Harding Fruit & Veg
107 D. Smith Grocer & Dairy
109 W.H Wood Butchers
111 Knitkraft Knit & Wool
113 Lawton's Baker
115 Toner & Williams Tobacconists
117 T.D Ambrose Chemist
119 Peacock Restaurant

1953

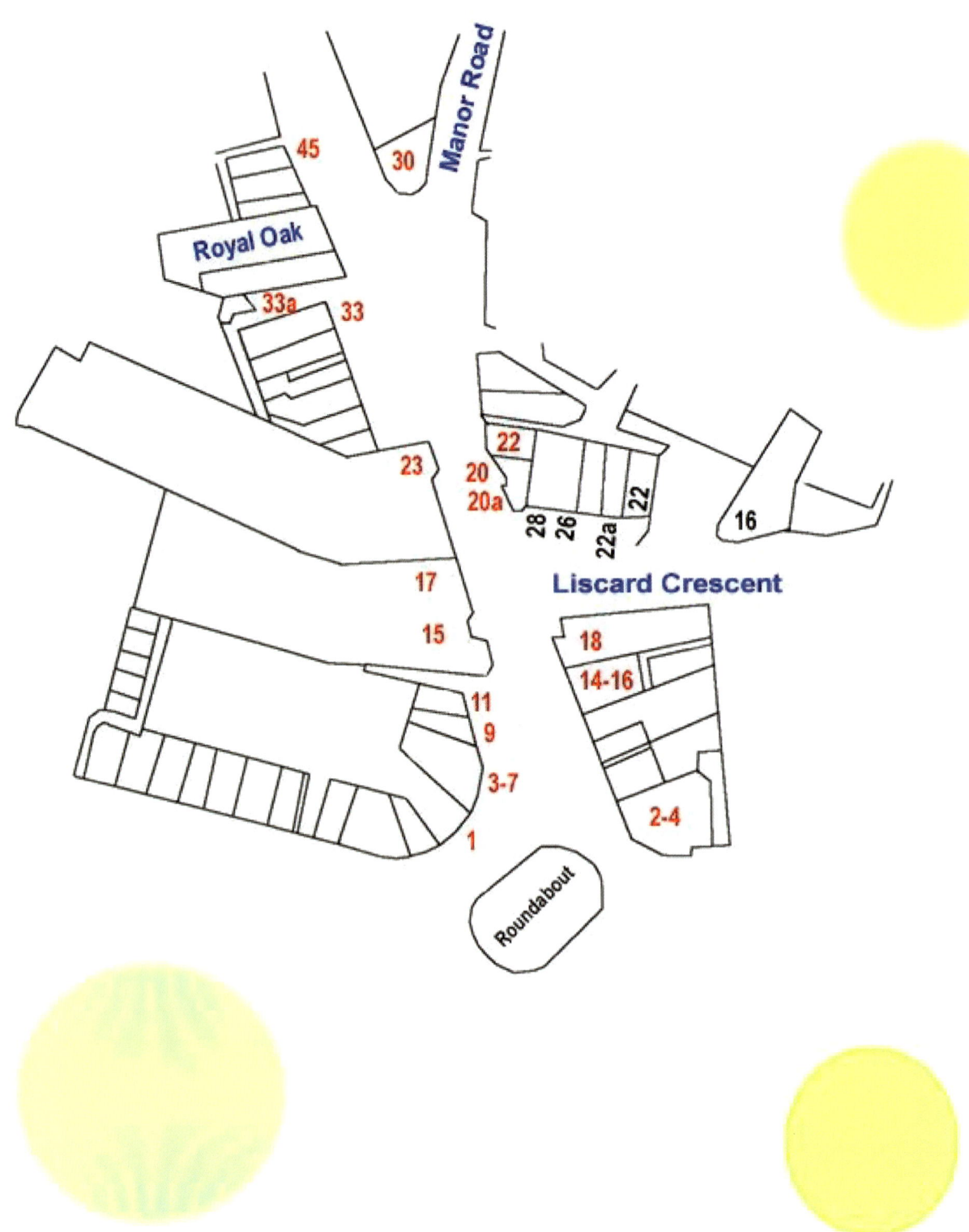

Liscard Village Trade Directory, 1967

1 Capitol Cinema
3-7 Barclays Bank
9 J. Lloyd & Son Footwear
11 R. Zalud Gowns
13-17 Ellison Brothers Ltd Wallpaper & Paint
19-23 Gibbons Undertakers
25 P.J. Pratley Carpet Dealers
25a County Borough of Wallasey Welfare Food Distributing Centre
27 Adrienne Ladies Hairdresser
29 W.H. Farrell Ltd Builders
31 J. Charles Dodd & Son Opticians
33 Royal Liver Friendly Assurance Society
33a Anthony Lockhart
33b Joe Brown Turf Commission Agents
35 The Salad Shop Greengrocers
39 Royal Oak
41 Messrs C&W Jones Woollen Drapers
43 Messrs H.& E.Brown Newsagents
45 Richard Breheny Boot & Shoe Repairers

Martin Bank Chambers:
2-4 Martins Bank
George E.Jones & Son Certified Accountants
Borough of Wallasey Butchers
Hannaford & Taggart Solicitors

6 George J. Mason Ltd Grocers

Central Chambers:
8 Pearl Assurance Co. Ltd

10 Marriots Tobacconists
12 George Young Pork Butchers
14-16 Telefusion Ltd TV Sales
18 National Provisional Bank
20a Exchange Mart Gentlemen Dealers
20a Joe Brown Turf Commission Agents
20b Haworth & Gallagher Solicitors
20 S. Hewlett Newsagent
22a Jones Bros. Fruiterer
24 Kenny Campbell Ltd Athletic Outfitters
26 Thomas Ewart Bell Butcher
Fire (Central) Station
30 Griffiths Chemist
Wallasey Post Office
Queen's Arms Pub

LISCARD

1966. View of the exterior of the Birkenhead Co-Op Store which opened in 1964. Once the largest department store in Wallasey. The Store was demolished by 1982 to make way for the food restaurant McDonalds.

1966. View of the interior of the First Floor of the Birkenhead Co-Op Store. Known as the Fashion Floor where you would find Lingerie and Children's Departments.

View of Liscard Road in 1966. At 286-288 Liscard Road on the left is Woolworths. The store opened in 1930 and served the local community for nearly 80 years.

A 1966 view of Wallasey Road. It was only a short time after that Liscard was to see a major development which included by 1982 the introduction of the one-way traffic system. On the right is Coronation Buildings which opened in 1938.

LISCARD

1934. The Electrical Showroom. Wallasey Road

1932. Triumph Auto Pianos. 283 Liscard Road

1927. Ellison Brothers. 15 Liscard Village

1937. Barber & Co. Wine Merchants. 223 Seaview Road

1963 Lennons Supermarket Seaview Road

LISCARD

1927. The Capitol Cinema opeend in 1926 and closed in 1974. By 1978 the building was in use ahain as for Bingo but by the 1990s had closed again.

1980. Liscard Town Centre. Looking towards Seaview Road with the Wellington Pub to the left.

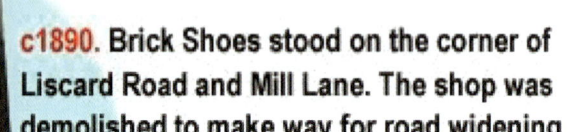

c1890. Brick Shoes stood on the corner of Liscard Road and Mill Lane. The shop was demolished to make way for road widening.

1953. Top of Seaview Road with Malpas Road straight to the left.

LISCARD

c1920. The original Boot Inn is pictured at the end of the row of buildings on the left. By 1924 the old pub was demolished and a new one built further back from the road.

1936. Wallasey Road with St. Alban's Road on the immediate right. The white building is May Cottage and next door was the pub Castle Hotel. The building standing centre in the distance was the old Wellington Pub, which was demolished a year later and a new one built further back from the road.

Early 1970's view of the newly developed modern Shopping Centre in Liscard. Work began in May 1968 to demolish all the houses in the area and many streets would disappear under modern shops and a car park

Another view of Liscard Shopping Centre from the early 1970's. Brand new stores soon opened which included TESCO, Telefusion, Radio Rentals and Sayers.

The Swiss word for fashion flair. Tissot.

Is your wrist doing anything for you? Tissot say it should, and show you how with new designs in 9 and 18ct gold.

These ladies' watches are original and beautiful – with shimmering bracelets to complete an elegant circle around your wrist.

Wear Tissot this year and you know that your watch is fashionable, and priced at a level which suits you, too – from £48.00 to £200.

Come and see the beauty of Tissot gold – in our showrooms now.

TISSOT
The Swiss watch the Swiss buy.

E. K. LAURIE LTD.
(Jewellers)
38-40 Seaview Road, Wallasey
Tel: 638 2795

1974 advert. Eric Laurie established his watch-maker business in 1914. The shop was originally at No. 114a Seaview Road but moved to the current premises in 1940

Unit Four Cinema

Once standing on the corner of King Street and Trafalgar Road stood an impressive 1930's style classical cinema. The history of a cinema located on this corner goes back to the early nineteenth century when the original picture house, which was once a Presbyterian church, opened in 1910 as the *Lyceum* showing the latest marvel of silent movies.

In March 1933 the building had to be demolished after a serious fire broke out in December 1931. By November 1933 the new 1,209 seating cinema was opened and named the *Gaumont* and was designed in a classical style.

4th May, 1976

By October 1974 the *Gaumont* had been bought by the *Unit Four Cinemas*. Within a few weeks of new owners the auditorium was split into four seperate cinemas and a licensed bar included and by 1979 two additional cinemas were added.

Apollo Leisure took over the cinema in 1994 and renamed it as Apollo 6. It was a short venture because by 2000 the cinema closed. The building was demoilshed in 2005.

THE STANLEY HOTEL,
76 Victoria Road, SEACOMBE
(Close to the Irving Theatre).
J. J. LINTON, Proprietor.

Highest Qualities of Scotch and Irish Whiskies.

BURTON ALES AT ORDINARY PRICES.

1907 advert of The Stanley Arms Hotel. The pub opened in 1839 at 76 Victoria Road (later renamed Borough Road), Seacombe. The pub closed by the 1980's.

COACH & HORSES HOTEL,
MORETON, CHESHIRE.
SYLVESTER S. MORRIS, Proprietor.

Allsopp's and West Cheshire Mild Ales always in Prime Condition.
Catering for Large and Small Parties on the Shortest Notice.
The Best of Everything at the Lowest Possible Price.
Sunday Evening Teas a Speciality.

1910 advert of the Coach & Horses, Moreton. The original pub was a tiny stone house and opened in the late 1600's.

In the 1920's Moreton was expanding so plans were made to build a new pub and in 1928 the current structure opened.

New Brighton BATHING POOL

BRITAIN'S FINEST WATER STADIUM

Swimming and Bathing for Adults and Kiddies in Ideal Surroundings.
ACCOMMODATION — 3,000 BATHERS, 20,000 SPECTATORS

THE EVENT OF THE SEASON !

3-0 p.m. EACH WEDNESDAY, 1st JULY to 12th AUGUST.
also SATURDAYS, 11th & 25th JULY and 8th AUGUST.
HEATS OF THE
"MISS NEW BRIGHTON 1953"
BATHING GIRL CONTEST.
Grand Final:—WEDNESDAY, 19th AUGUST.
Full Details from:—Entertainments Manager, Town Hall, Wallasey.

Saturdays, September 5th, 12th, 19th, 1953 — 9-0 p.m.
BROCK'S
GIGANTIC FIREWORKS DISPLAYS
ADMISSION — Adults 1/- :: Children 6d.

General Admission to Pool — 6d.

Construction of the Open Air Baths
New Brighton
1934

Construction of the dressing block

13.04.1934

Looking north east from deep end

17.11.1933

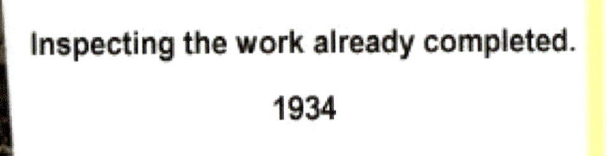

Inspecting the work already completed.

1934

View of the interior toward the tier.

25.05.1934

Opening of the Open Air Baths
New Brighton
19th June 1934

Opening ceremony

1934

View of slide and admin block

1934

View of the fountain

1934

The changing cubicles

1934

THE T★O★W★E★R

1953

Merseyside's Mecca of Entertainment

Ballroom
"The Dancers' Paradise"
Dancing to
BERT YATES and his
"TOWER RHYTHMICS"
Special Attractions ! !
See Adverts.

Amusement Park
Largest and Best
THRILLING RIDES
GAMES · AUTOMATICS
CHILDREN'S PLAYGROUND
MINIATURE RAILWAYS

Visit the Latest Thriller

THE HAUNTED CASTLE

★ ★ ★

CATERING AND LICENSED BARS

Cafeteria
GOOD FOOD
QUICK SERVICE
POPULAR PRICES

Restaurant
PERFECT MEALS
IDEAL SURROUNDINGS
WAITER SERVICE

Lakeside Bar
(Adjoining Cafeteria)

BEERS · WINES
SPIRITS

Rock Point Bar
(Adjoining Restaurant)
BEERS · WINES · SPIRITS
COCKTAILS
New Brighton's Latest Highspot
Open Daily until 10 p.m.

THEATRE — STADIUM

Boxing
Every Monday at 7.30 p.m.
FIRST-CLASS PROGRAMMES
Seats bookable in advance
Popular Prices

Wrestling
Every Wednesday at 7.30 p.m.
ALL STAR PROGRAMMES
Seats bookable in advance
Popular Prices

Printed in Great Britain
by Amazon